Here I Am!

MY FIRST FUN JEWISH JOURNAL

I0157271

Name _____

Date of Birth _____ Age _____

Date I started this journal _____

Jewish School _____ City _____

My favorite things to do _____

_____

Table of Contents

What's in my name?

My English name is _____

It means _____

I like/don't like it because _____

My Hebrew name is _____

It means _____

I like/don't like it because _____

I can write it with Hebrew letters like this: _____

These are my namesakes — the people I'm named for:

Namesake _____	Namesake _____
He/she was my _____	He/she was my _____
I'm named for him/her because _____ _____	I'm named for him/her because _____ _____
My name is: ❑ exactly like my namesake's ❑ different but has the same first letter	My name is: ❑ exactly like my namesake's ❑ different but has the same first letter
Namesake _____	Namesake _____
He/she was my _____	He/she was my _____
I'm named for him/her because _____ _____	I'm named for him/her because _____ _____
My name is: ❑ exactly like my namesake's ❑ different but has the same first letter	My name is: ❑ exactly like my namesake's ❑ different but has the same first letter

In these two frames, draw pictures of your namesakes. If you don't have photos of them, what do you think they looked like?

I WISH I HAD KNOWN MY GREAT-GRANDFATHER — WE HAVE THE SAME NAME!

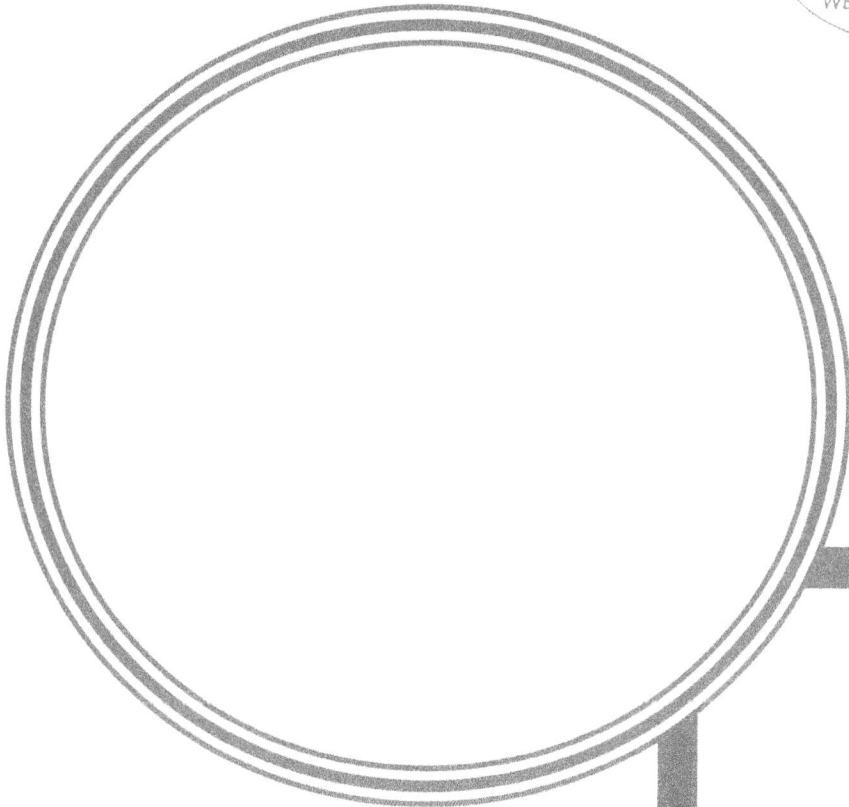

This person
☐ was alive   ☐ was not alive
when I was born.

Here's a drawing of what my name means:

This person
☐ was alive   ☐ was not alive
when I was born.

Dear Diary,

My favorite things about the new year are

_____

_____

_____

_____

_____

School started and _____

_____

_____

_____

The weather has been _____

_____

_____

My family _____

_____

_____

_____

I went to _____

_____

_____

_____

_____

_____

ELUL / TISHRI

- Go to services
- Miss school
- Eat apples and honey

Dear Diary,

In this class I am learning about _____

_____

_____

_____

_____

ELUL / TISHRI

- Think about the past year
- Build a sukkah
- Dance with the Torah

Shabbat is special when _____

_____

_____

_____

_____

On Sukkot we _____

_____

_____

_____

I'm looking forward to _____

MITZVAH MEMO

I apologized to _____

_____

for _____

_____

_____

_____

_____

High Holy Days

On Rosh HaShanah, we think of things we did in the past year that we wish we could "throw away." At the Tashlich ceremony, we throw bread crumbs into a river to symbolize these things.

Things I could get rid of:

Toys _____

Books _____

Videos _____

Games _____

Clothes _____

HOW CAN YOU THROW AWAY SOMETHING THAT YOU ALREADY DID?

I JUST WANT TO THROW AWAY THE BAD FEELINGS THAT WERE LEFT.

Feelings I don't need anymore:

Sadness I felt when _____

_____

_____

Anger I felt when _____

_____

_____

Embarrassment I felt when _____

_____

_____

Bad habits I'd like to throw away:

_____

_____

_____

More Jews go to synagogue during the High Holy Days than at any other time of the year.

I've been to synagogue for:

☐ **Rosh HaShanah**

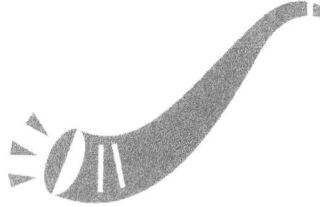

☐ **Yom Kippur**

☐ **Shabbat**

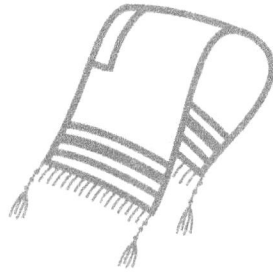

☐ **Bar/Bat Mitzvah**

☐ **Simchat Torah**

☐ **Shavuot**

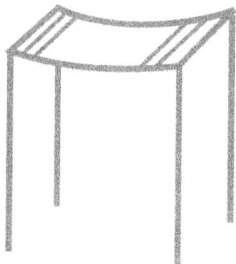

☐ **Wedding**

☐ **Funeral**

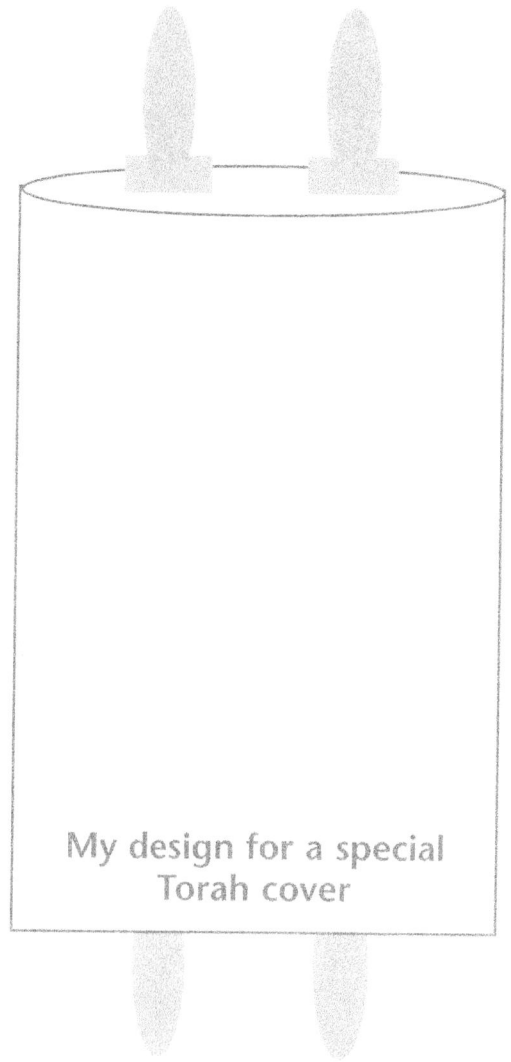

My design for a special Torah cover

What I've done in synagogue:

☐ Followed along in Hebrew

☐ Followed along in English

☐ Sang a song

☐ Kissed the Torah

☐ Wore a kipah

☐ Heard the shofar

☐ Stood up and sat down at the right times

☐ Went to a children's service

☐ _____

What's in my synagogue?

How many of each of these things can you find in your synagogue? Count them and write the number in the box by each picture.

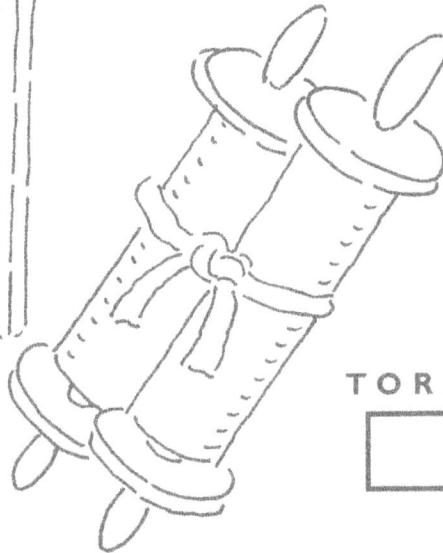

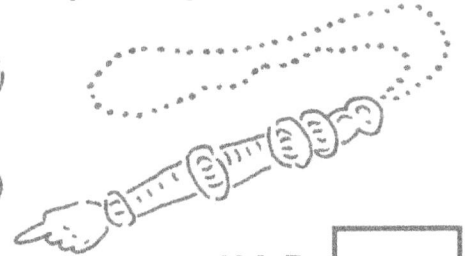

YAD [ ]

ARK [ ]

TORAH [ ]

KIPAH [ ]

BJMAH [ ]

SIDDUR [ ]

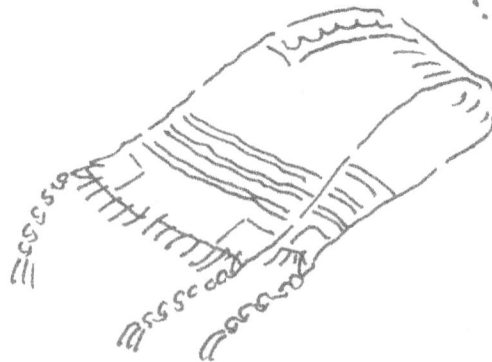

TALLIT [ ]

BREASTPLATE [ ]

RIMMONIM [ ]

CHUMASH [ ]

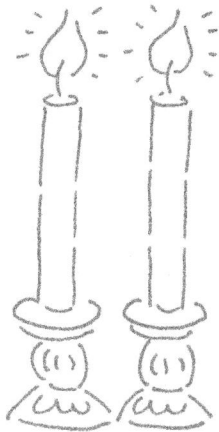

CANDLES [ ]

NER TAMID [ ]

KIDDUSH CUP [ ]

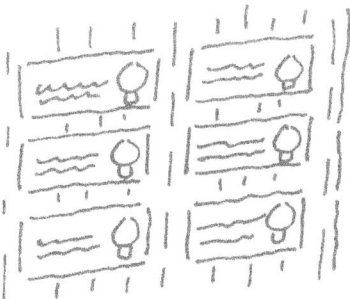

MEMORIAL WALL [ ]

MECHITZAH [ ]

My synagogue also has:

- [ ] Rabbi (how many? _____)
- [ ] Cantor
- [ ] Youth Group
- [ ] Choir
- [ ] Seniors Group
- [ ] Women's Group
- [ ] Men's Group
- [ ] Adult Education classes
- [ ] Shabbat services
- [ ] Tot Shabbat
- [ ] Kitchen
- [ ] Cook
- [ ] Office staff
- [ ] Custodian
- [ ] Junior Youth Group
- [ ] Holocaust Torah
- [ ] _____

9

Modeh Ani

There's a thank-you prayer for Jewish children to say when we wake up in the morning:

וְקַיָּם, שֶׁהֶחֱזַרְתָּ בִּי נִשְׁמָתִי בְּחֶמְלָה, רַבָּה אֱמוּנָתֶךָ.

It means, "Thank you, God, for giving my soul back to me."

When I wake up in the morning, I feel (circle one or more):

 tired

 grumpy

 lonely

 happy

 healthy

 sick

 mischievous

Most mornings, I look forward to _____

_____

_____

Some mornings, I feel worried about _____

_____

When I wake up, I might say thank you to God for _____

_____

_____

This is a drawing of a dream I remember:

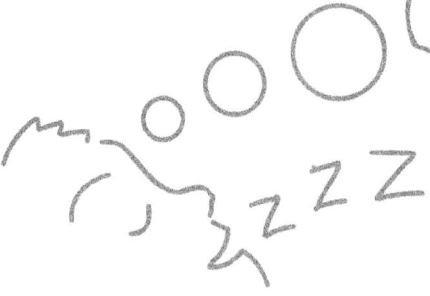

When I am sleeping, _____

_____

_____

Where is my family from?

Draw a happy face ☺ on this map where you live.

Find out where your family members came from and mark them on the map. (Use a detailed world map if you need more information.) Use M for mother, F for father, G for grandparents, and GG for great-grandparents.

Did anyone in your family emigrate from another country? Draw a line that shows their journey.

What's in my house?

How many of these Jewish objects are in your house? Circle the ones you can find. Decorate them with your own designs.

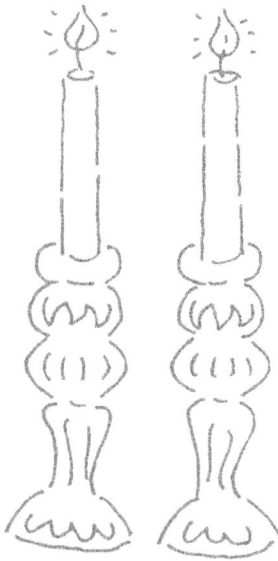

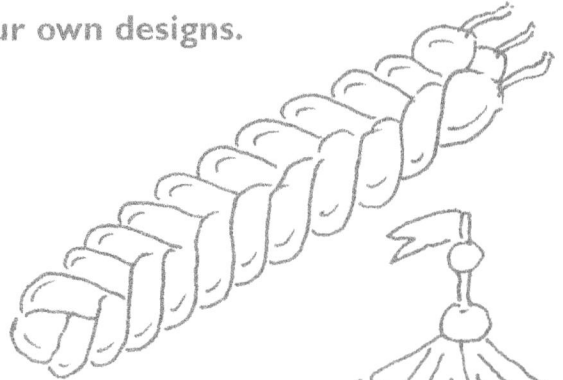

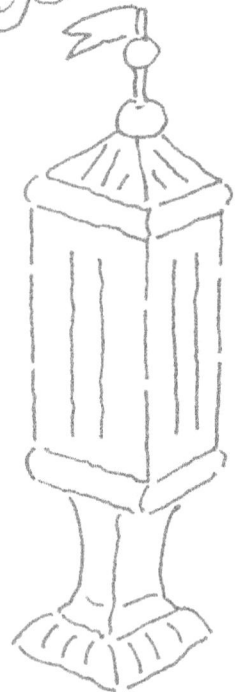

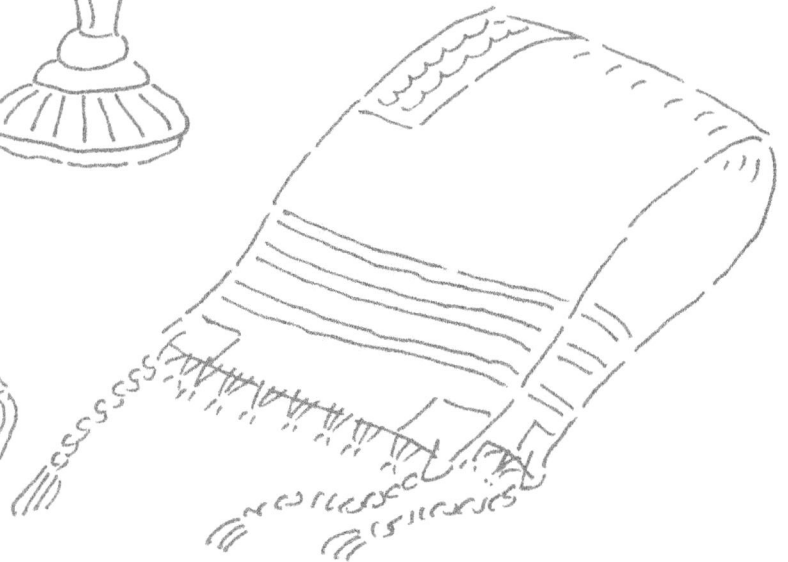

צדקה

תורה

How many of these objects did you find?

- ❑ Shabbat candlesticks
- ❑ Tzedakah box
- ❑ Kiddush cup
- ❑ Challah cover
- ❑ Mezuzah (how many? ___)
- ❑ Prayer book
- ❑ Kippot (how many? ___)
- ❑ Tallitot (how many? ___)
- ❑ Chanukiah
- ❑ Seder plate
- ❑ Havdalah candle
- ❑ Spice box
- ❑ Matzah cover
- ❑ Handwashing cup
- ❑ Tanach (Jewish Bible)

MITZVAH MEMO

I used _____

_____

when I performed
a mitzvah at home.

Dear Diary,

My favorite things about this season are

_____

_____

_____

_____

_____

At school we _____

_____

_____

_____

The weather has been _____

_____

_____

My friend(s) and I _____

_____

_____

_____

For Thanksgiving I _____

_____

_____

_____

CHESHVAN / KISLEV

- Light Chanukah candles
- Help make latkes
- Play Dreidel

Dear Diary,

In this class I learned about _____

_____

_____

_____

_____

_____

Shabbat is special when _____

_____

_____

_____

_____

_____

On Chanukah we _____

_____

_____

_____

_____

I'm looking forward to _____

_____

_____

_____

_____

_____

CHESHVAN / KISLEV
- Give and receive gifts
- Gather with family
- Sing songs

MITZVAH MEMO

On Chanukah I _____

_____

_____

_____

_____

Chanukah

Chanukah means "dedication." The Maccabees rededicated the Temple in Jerusalem to make it holy. That Temple no longer exists, but our homes can be holy places.

Draw or write about some of the holy things you can do in your home.

Could these be holy activities?

- ❏ Eating together
- ❏ Reading
- ❏ Studying
- ❏ Saying blessings
- ❏ Special family time
- ❏ Bedtime
- ❏ Waking up
- ❏ Lighting candles
- ❏ _____
- ❏ _____

The letters on a dreidel stand for the words "a great miracle happened there."

The miracle was _____

_____

_____

I ❑ believe ❑ don't believe that miracles can happen in our time.

I believe: ❑ God makes miracles happen.

❑ People make miracles happen.

❑ Sometimes amazing things just happen.

**Here's a miraculous thing that happened to me
this past year (draw or write about it):**

*I GOT A NEW
ADOPTED COUSIN
THIS YEAR!*

*MY UNCLE GOT
SICK, BUT HE'S
GETTING BETTER!*

My Winter Thoughts and Feelings

Most people in the world celebrate winter holidays during the month of December.

In the winter, most of my friends celebrate _____

That ❑ is ❑ isn't the same holiday I celebrate.

That makes me feel _____

_____

Getting presents at this time of year ❑ is ❑ isn't very important to me.

	AGREE	DISAGREE
I need a lot more stuff.	❑	❑
A gift is something you have to buy.	❑	❑
A gift is the best way to show you love someone.	❑	❑

To whom would you like to give a special gift?
Draw the gift here.

I'D LIKE TO GIVE MY GRANDMA A BUNCH OF PLANE TICKETS SO SHE COULD VISIT ME A LOT!

Winter holidays bring out many different feelings.

This is how I feel:

I'M JEWISH AND SOME OF MY FRIENDS AREN'T.

I'M JEWISH AND ALL MY FRIENDS ARE JEWISH. WE ALL CELEBRATE CHANUKAH.

MY FAMILY CELEBRATES TWO HOLIDAYS IN DECEMBER.

I WISH EVERYBODY WOULD CELEBRATE CHANUKAH WITH ME.

I LIKE TO LOOK AT LIGHTS EVEN THOUGH I KNOW THEY'RE NOT FOR MY HOLIDAY.

I LOVE CHANUKAH! IT'S MY FAVORITE HOLIDAY.

I LOVE MAKING PRESENTS FOR MY FRIENDS!

I'M SAD IF I DON'T GET LOTS OF PRESENTS.

Draw yourself here with your favorite Chanukah object.

The Shema

This is one of the most important Jewish prayers:

שְׁמַע יִשְׂרָאֵל יְיָ אֱלֹהֵינוּ, יְיָ אֶחָד.

It means, "Listen, Israel, Adonai is our God, Adonai is One."

I ❑ have ❑ have not heard this prayer before.

The Shema is said many times a day. I've heard it at:

_____

_____

Shema means "Listen!" I like to listen to _____

_____

_____

I don't like to listen to _____

_____

_____

DO YOU THINK GOD LISTENS TO YOU?

To me, "God is One" means _____

_____

_____

_____

These are some questions I have about God:

_____

_____

_____

_____

_____

Of course, no one can draw a picture of God.
But can you draw a picture *about* God?

If I could write a note
to God at bedtime
I would say:

Dear God,

_____

_____

_____

_____

_____

_____

signed,

_____

Are there times when God

make things happen in my life?

is near?

Are there places where

Does God

God feels closer?

Many Jewish children say the Shema before they go to sleep.
Color in the thoughts you have before you fall asleep.

I'm scared.

I'm excited about tomorrow.

I'm not tired!

I like to sleep with my _____

I wish I had done better at _____ today.

_____
_____

Shabbat

The first book of the Torah tells us that God created the world in six days and rested on the seventh day. We, too, are told to rest on Shabbat.

Which of these activities involve working and which involve resting?

	WORK	REST	NOT SURE
Going to school	❏	❏	❏
Cooking	❏	❏	❏
Doing homework	❏	❏	❏
Playing soccer	❏	❏	❏
Playing chess	❏	❏	❏
Watching TV	❏	❏	❏
Riding a bike	❏	❏	❏
Riding in a car	❏	❏	❏
Being on vacation	❏	❏	❏
Praying	❏	❏	❏
Reading	❏	❏	❏
Painting a picture	❏	❏	❏
Painting furniture	❏	❏	❏
Walking the dog	❏	❏	❏
Taking a nap	❏	❏	❏

To make Shabbat a special time, my family _____

_____

_____

_____

Here are some other things I'd like to do on Shabbat:

_____

_____

_____

_____

There's a tradition that angels of peace visit us on Shabbat. On Friday night we sing the song "Shalom Aleichem" to welcome these angels of peace.

**Draw a scene you'd like an angel of peace
to see in your house on Friday night:**

Sh'lom Bayit (Peace in the Home)

The root of the Hebrew word *shalom* means "completeness."

My home feels peaceful or complete when _____

_____

_____

My home doesn't feel peaceful or complete when _____

_____

_____

Dear Diary,

My favorite things about winter are _____

_____

_____

_____

_____

The weather has been _____

_____

_____

For winter break I _____

_____

_____

_____

_____

_____

A person who is special to me _____

_____

_____

_____

_____

_____

_____

TEVET / SHEVAT

- Get cozy and read a Jewish book

- Share a book with a friend

Dear Diary,

In this class I learned about _____

_____

_____

_____

_____

Shabbat is special when _____

_____

_____

_____

_____

On Tu B'Shevat we _____

_____

_____

_____

_____

TEVET / SHEVAT
- Plant some seeds
- Eat special fruits
- Take a nature walk

MITZVAH MEMO

I helped the earth by

_____

_____

_____

I'm looking forward to _____

_____

_____

_____

_____

_____

My Hands

On special occasions, Jewish women from some countries decorate their hands and feet with henna, a red coloring. Here's how I'd like to decorate my hands:

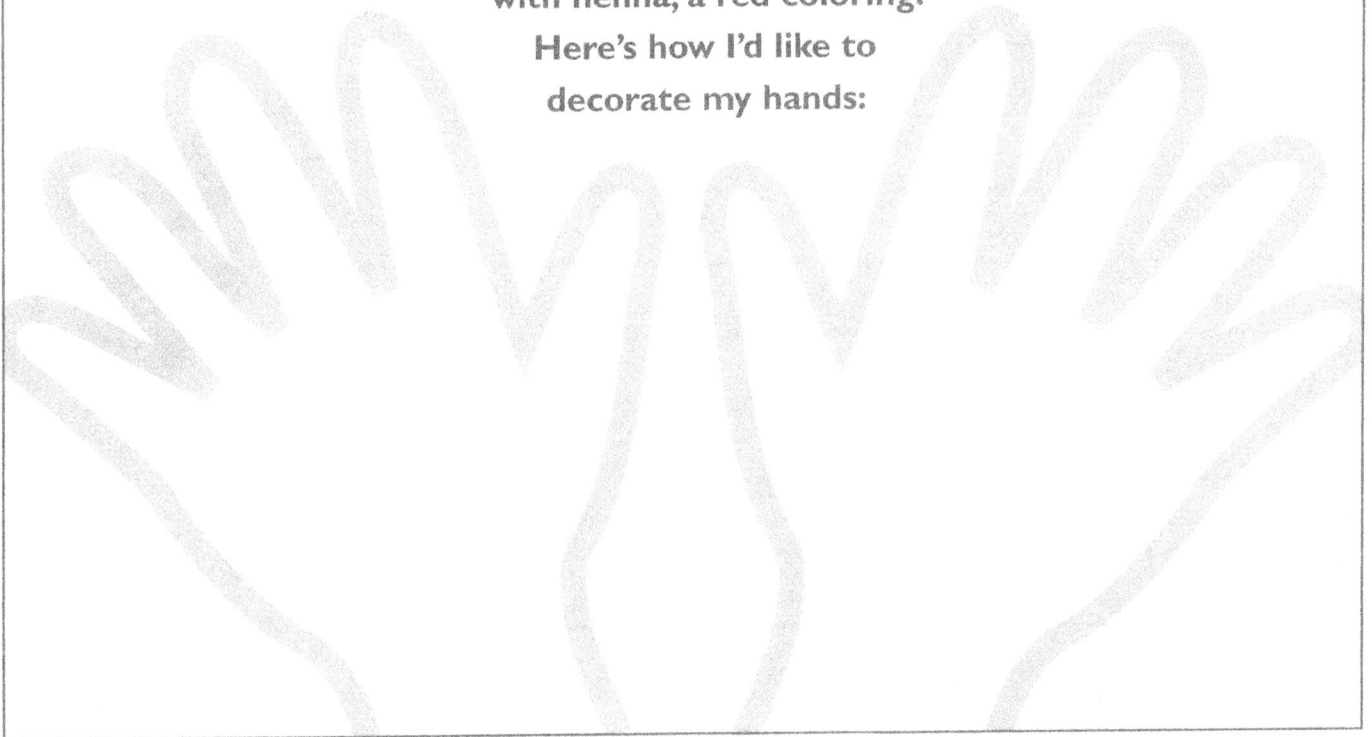

I can do lots of mitzvot with my hands, like

_____

_____

_____

_____

_____

_____

_____

THAT'S A WEIRD-LOOKING HAND!

IT'S A HAMSA — SOME PEOPLE THINK IT BRINGS GOOD LUCK.

My Feet

This is a drawing of my favorite pair of shoes.

These are Jewish places my feet can take me:

_____

_____

_____

_____

_____

_____

_____

My house feels like a Jewish place when

_____

_____

My school feels like a Jewish place when

_____

_____

My favorite restaurant could be a Jewish place if _____

_____

Being a Mensch

A great teacher named Hillel told us that in a place where there is no mensch, you should try to be a mensch. A mensch is a decent person — one who treats others well.

What does it mean to be a mensch? Judaism gives us many helpful rules. Some of them are commandments written in the Torah. Others come later from Rabbis and teachers. Here are a few Jewish rules for being a good person:

FOR ME, THIS RULE IS . . .	EASY TO FOLLOW	HARD TO FOLLOW
Honor your parents.	❏	❏
Don't steal.	❏	❏
Don't be jealous of what other people have.	❏	❏
Don't use bad language.	❏	❏
Take care of animals.	❏	❏
Don't talk about others behind their back.	❏	❏
Visit sick people.	❏	❏
Don't embarrass people.	❏	❏
Don't judge people by how they look.	❏	❏

The easiest rule to follow is _____

_____

because _____

_____

The hardest rule to follow is _____

_____

because _____

_____

EVERYONE'S BEEN TEASING ME ABOUT MY NEW BRACES EXCEPT YOU!

MAYBE THEY FORGOT WHAT IT MEANS TO BE A MENSCH!

Draw a cartoon of yourself following one of these Jewish rules.

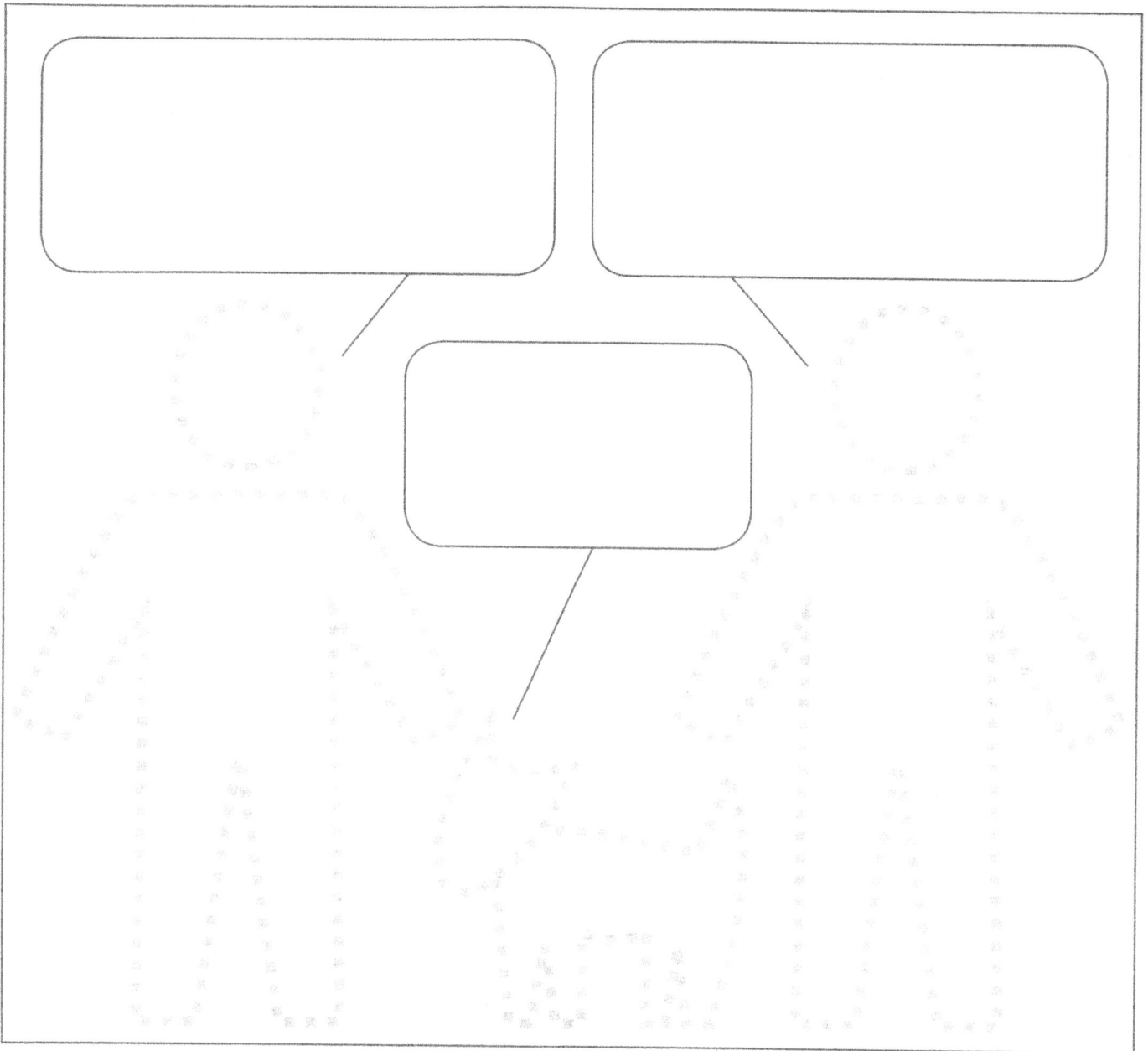

Have you ever been somewhere when someone wasn't behaving like a mensch?

How it made me feel:_____

_____

I was behaving _____

_____

Maybe next time I would _____

_____

I'm a tree!

I'm like a tree getting nourishment from my roots. My roots are all the people in my family who came before me.

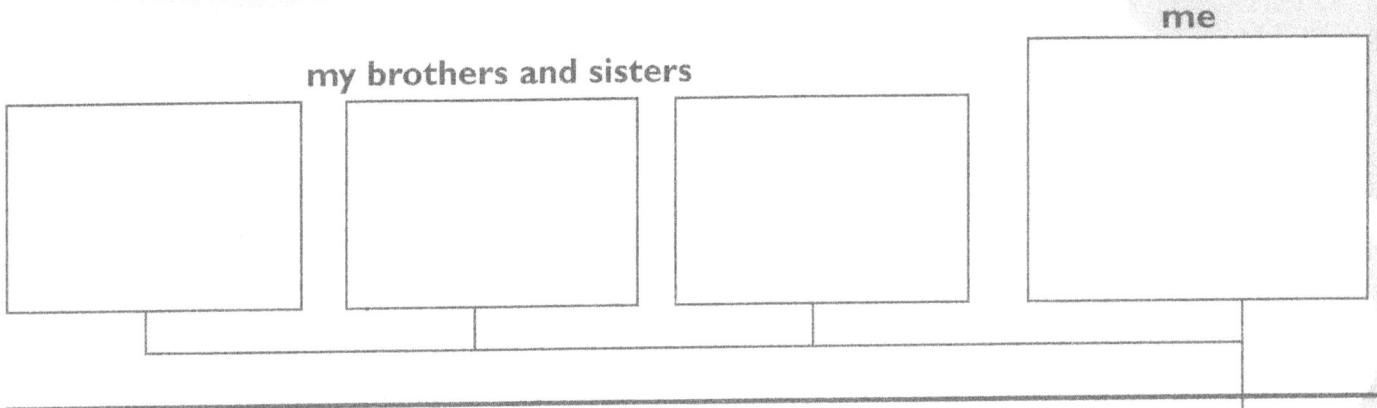

me

my brothers and sisters

Ask your parents to help you fill in the names of your roots.

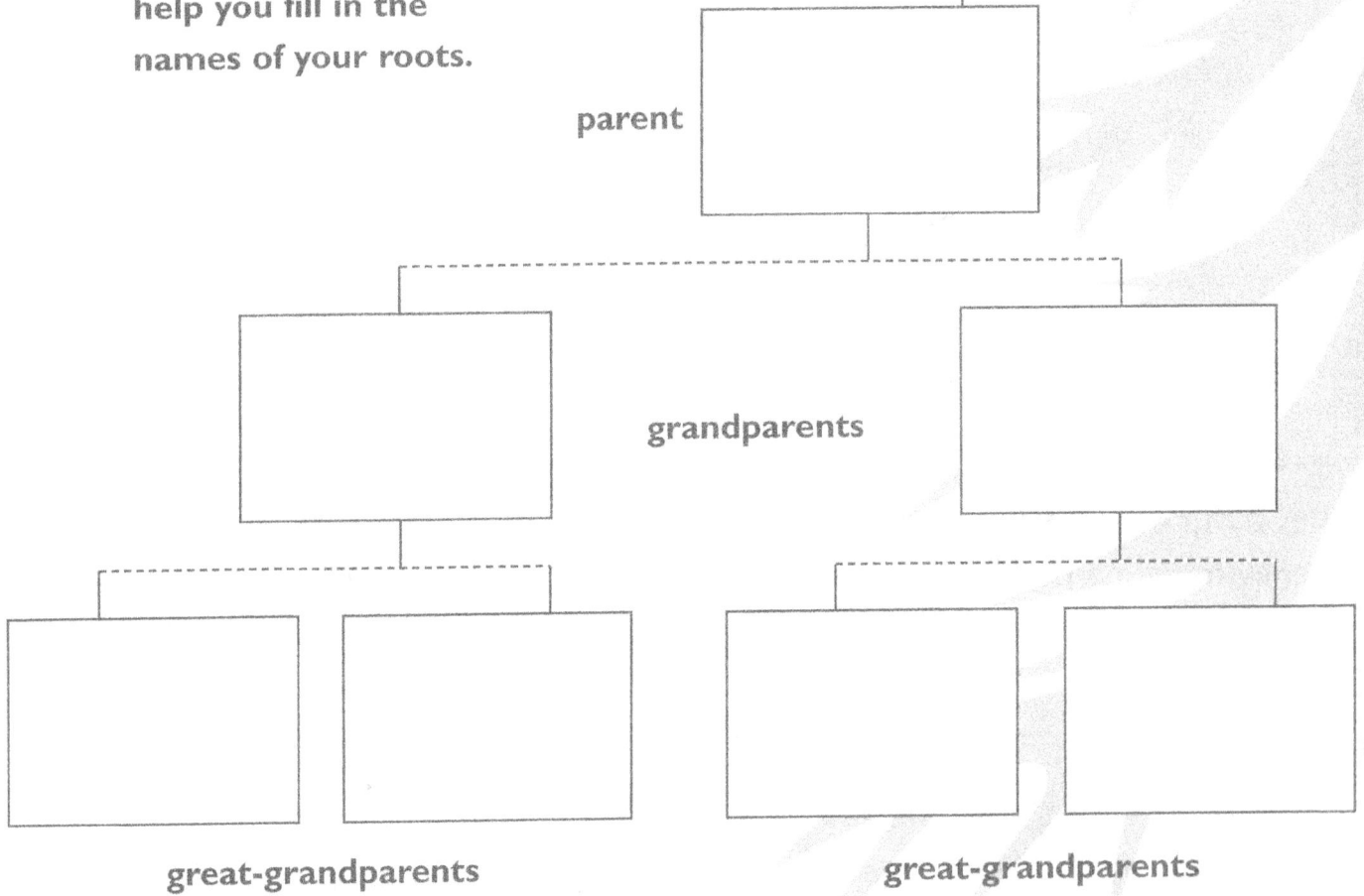

parent

grandparents

great-grandparents

great-grandparents

I HAVE EIGHT GRANDPARENTS!

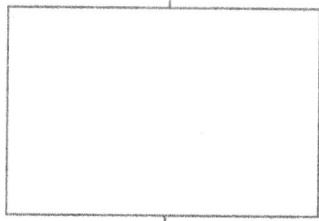

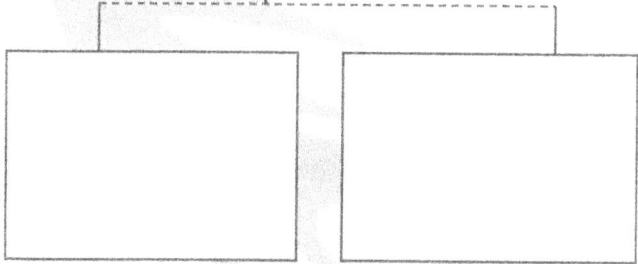

WOW — YOU HAVE LOTS OF ROOTS!

The Torah is called a tree of life. How is a person like a Torah?

_____

_____

_____

_____

_____

_____

parent

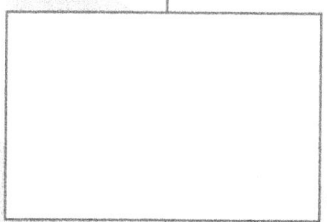

grandparents

great-grandparents

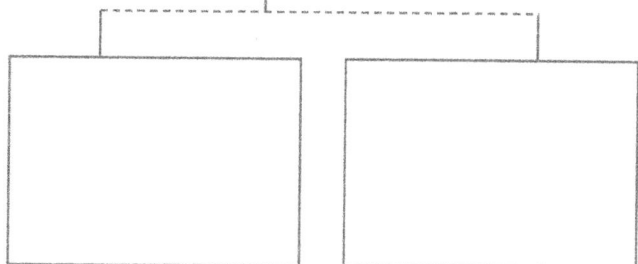

great-grandparents

Shehecheyanu

There is a prayer we say for special times and new beginnings:

בָּרוּךְ אַתָּה יְיָ אֱלֹהֵינוּ מֶלֶךְ הָעוֹלָם שֶׁהֶחֱיָנוּ וְקִיְּמָנוּ וְהִגִּיעָנוּ לַזְּמַן הַזֶּה.

The first time I walked I was _____ years old, and I

_____.

The first time I talked I was _____ years old, and I

_____.

The first time I swam I was _____ years old, and I

_____.

The first time I read a book I was _____ years old, and I

_____.

The first time I rode a bike I was _____ years old, and I

_____.

The first time I lit Shabbat candles I was _____ years old, and I

_____.

The first time I said "HaMotzi" I was _____ years old, and I

_____.

The first time I lit Chanukah candles I was _____ years old, and I

_____.

The first time I went to a Bar or Bat Mitzvah I was _____ years old, and I _____.

WHERE WERE YOU?
WHO WAS WITH YOU?
HOW DID IT FEEL?

I DON'T REMEMBER —
I'LL ASK MY MOM!

What do you remember about some first times from this year?

The first time I ate a special food

_____

The first night of a holiday

_____

The first time I wore new clothes

_____

The first day of school

_____

I've done these special things (circle the ones you've done):

see the ocean

go to the mountains

fly in an airplane

visit another country

see a shooting star

watch a sunrise

sleep in a tent

see a rainbow

The next time you do any of these things, remember to say a "Shehecheyanu." Some of these events even have their own special blessing.

Creating Our World

When we sing a song, draw a picture, play an instrument, solve a problem, or write a story, we're being creative. When we use the talents and abilities God gave us, we are helping God with the work of creation.

A creative thing that I did was _____

_____

I got the idea from _____

_____

As I was working on it, I felt _____

_____

When I was finished, I felt _____

_____

Can these be creative?

	YES	NO	MAYBE
Making a sandwich	❑	❑	❑
Acting in a play	❑	❑	❑
Baking challah	❑	❑	❑
Watching TV	❑	❑	❑
Taking a picture	❑	❑	❑
Writing a poem	❑	❑	❑
Saying a brachah	❑	❑	❑
Decorating a room	❑	❑	❑
Making up a song	❑	❑	❑

Many Jews have gotten inspiration for their art from Torah and other holy books. Use the words from one of these Hebrew quotes to make a design on the pattern below. (You might recognize the words from songs you know.)

הִנֵּה מַה טּוֹב וּמַה נָּעִים שֶׁבֶת אַחִים גַּם יָחַד.

How good and pleasant when people live together.

עֹשֶׂה שָׁלוֹם בִּמְרוֹמָיו הוּא יַעֲשֶׂה שָׁלוֹם

עָלֵינוּ וְעַל כָּל יִשְׂרָאֵל. וְאִמְרוּ אָמֵן.

May the One who makes peace in the heavens make peace for us and for all Israel, and we say amen.

Here is an example of a design made from Hebrew words. Can you recognize this blessing?

MAKING A DESIGN WITH TINY LETTERS IS CALLED MICROGRAPHY.

Dear Diary,

My favorite things about this season are

_____

_____

_____

_____

_____

At school we _____

_____

_____

_____

The weather has been _____

_____

_____

My family _____

_____

_____

_____

For Purim I _____

_____

_____

_____

_____

ADAR / NISAN
- Make a costume
- Eat hamentaschen
- Listen for "you-know-who"

Dear Diary,

I am learning about these Jewish things:

_____

_____

_____

_____

_____

What I like about Passover is _____

_____

_____

_____

_____

At the Seder I _____

_____

_____

_____

_____

I'm looking forward to _____

_____

_____

_____

_____

_____

ADAR / NISAN
- Practice the 4 questions
- Search for chametz
- Eat matzah

MITZVAH MEMO

I helped _____

_____

by _____

_____

Purim

Purim tells an exciting story with heroes, heroines, and villains. When you dress up like the Purim characters, what would it really be like to *be* them?

Hello! My name is Esther

My scariest moment was _____

_____

_____

Hello! My name is Mordechai

I wanted Esther to be queen because _____

_____

_____

Hello! My name is Vashti

I didn't go to the king's party because I felt

_____

_____

Hello! My name is Ahasuerus

When Esther told me she was really a Jew, I felt

_____

_____

Hello! My name is HAMAN

The reason I behave so badly is because

_____

_____

Do you ever put on a "mask" to hide how you really feel?
Like trying to look brave when you're really feeling scared or shy?

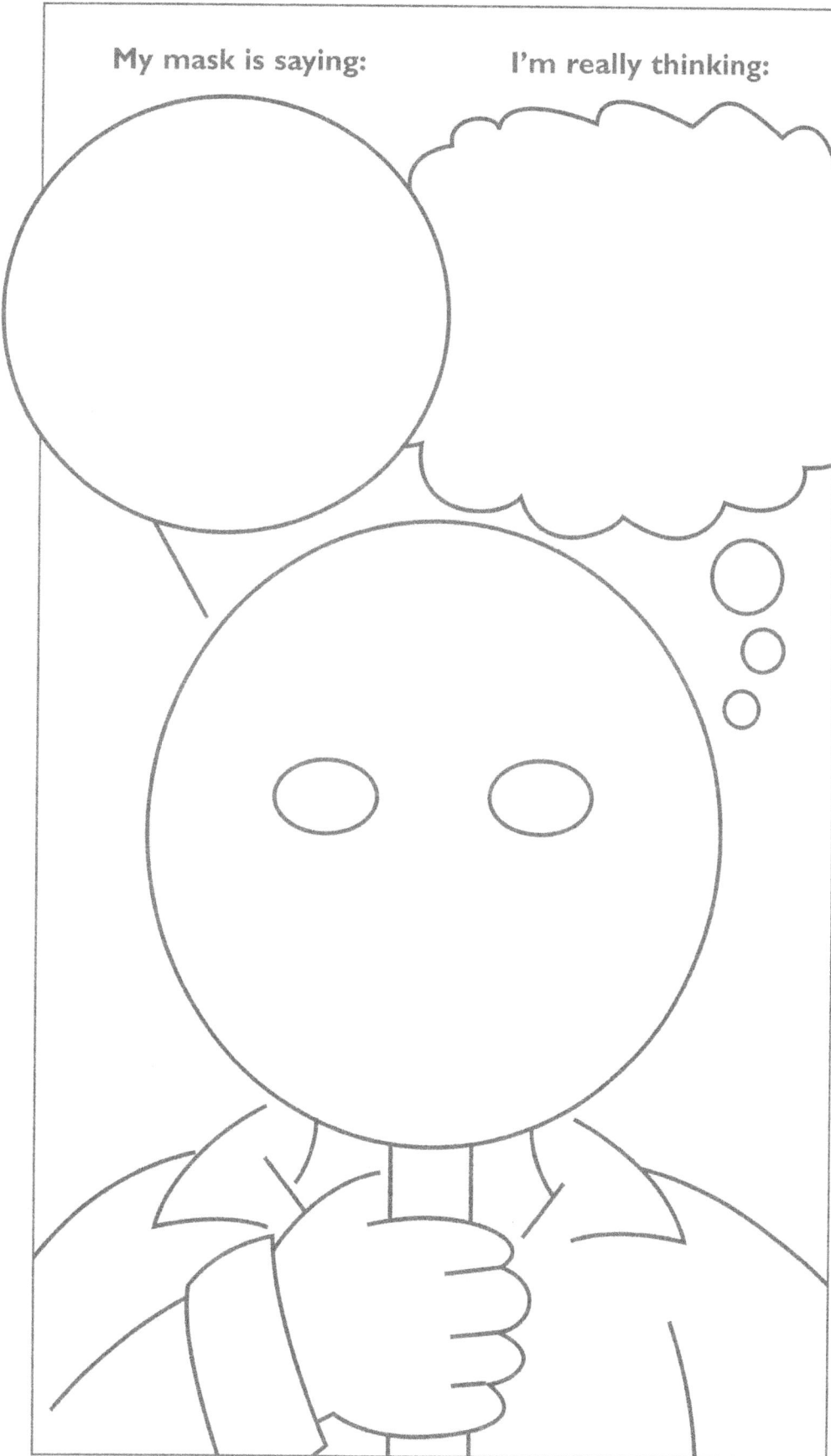

My mask is saying:

I'm really thinking:

Circle the "masks" that you sometimes put on.

brave

angry

smart

dumb

serious

goofy

I don't care

41

Pesach

In my family _____
leads the Seder. The kids participate by: _____
_____
_____
_____
_____

AT OUR SEDER I ATE A HILLEL SANDWICH.

I INVENTED A SANDWICH ONCE, BUT MY MOM WOULDN'T LET ME EAT IT.

My favorite part of the Seder is
_____
_____
_____
_____
because _____
_____

Things I do at Pesach:

- ❏ Eat a Hillel sandwich
- ❏ Eat a submarine sandwich
- ❏ Sing special songs
- ❏ Watch the World Series
- ❏ Search for buried treasure
- ❏ Search for the afikomen
- ❏ Recite the Four Questions
- ❏ Recite the Pledge of Allegiance
- ❏ Dress up in costumes
- ❏ Drink four milkshakes
- ❏ Drink four glasses of wine
- ❏ Open the door for Elijah
- ❏ Open the door for the mailman

A Fun Pesach Activity

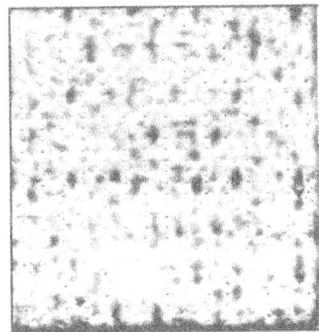

CAN YOU NIBBLE A PIECE OF MATZAH INTO A PERFECT CIRCLE?

IT'S HARD TO DO WITHOUT BREAKING THE MATZAH!

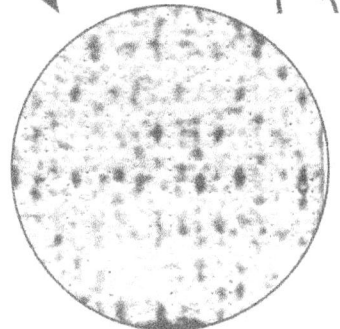

In the Exodus story, the Torah tells us that God punished Pharaoh and the Egyptians for not letting the Hebrews go free. Do you think the punishment was:

❑ too easy?   ❑ too harsh?   ❑ just right ?

Why? _____

_____

_____

_____

	AGREE	DISAGREE
People should be punished for doing wrong.	❑	❑
Bad things can happen to bad people.	❑	❑
Bad things can happen to good people.	❑	❑
Good things can happen to bad people.	❑	❑
Good things can happen to good people.	❑	❑
God punishes bad people.	❑	❑
God rewards good people.	❑	❑

A Time I Was Punished

When I was _____ years old I was punished for

_____

My punishment was

_____

I thought that was ❑ fair ❑ not fair

because

_____

My Friends

וְאָהַבְתָּ לְרֵעֲךָ כָּמוֹךָ.

You shall love your friend as yourself. (Leviticus)

My good friend's name is _____

We have been friends since _____

We met _____

_____

Things I like about my friend:

_____

_____

_____

Here's a drawing of me with my friend.

I have:

❑ An older friend

❑ A younger friend

❑ An animal friend

❑ A toy friend

❑ An imaginary friend

❑ A teacher friend

❑ A school friend

❑ A neighborhood friend

❑ A synagogue friend

❑ A sports friend

❑ A friend in my family

Can you think of any famous Jewish friends? Draw or write about them here.

I think a friend should be:

	YES	NO	NOT IMPORTANT
Honest	❑	❑	❑
Funny	❑	❑	❑
Rich	❑	❑	❑
Good looking	❑	❑	❑
Easy to talk to	❑	❑	❑
Loyal	❑	❑	❑
Gossipy	❑	❑	❑
Serious	❑	❑	❑
Jewish	❑	❑	❑
Into sports	❑	❑	❑
Perfect	❑	❑	❑
Generous	❑	❑	❑
Nearby	❑	❑	❑
A lot like me	❑	❑	❑

I TRY TO BE A GOOD FRIEND, BUT SOMETIMES I FORGET!

I REALLY LIKE IT WHEN YOU TRY!

MITZVAH MEMO

I was a good friend when I _____

_____

_____

_____

Autographs

How many of these autographs can you get?

my mother	my father
a sister	a sister
a brother	a brother
a grandmother	a grandmother
a grandfather	a grandfather
an aunt	an aunt
an uncle	an uncle
a cousin	a cousin
a friend	a friend

_____ my teacher

_____ my Hebrew teacher

_____ my Rabbi

_____ my Cantor

_____ a Hebrew reader

_____ a Torah reader

_____ someone who heals people

_____ someone who helps people

_____ someone who bakes challah

_____ someone who recites the Kiddush

_____ someone who can sound the shofar

_____ someone who fasts on Yom Kippur

_____ someone who has been to Israel

_____ someone who knows the alef-bet in order

_____ someone who was born in a different country

I DIDN'T KNOW YOU KNEW THE ALEF-BET!

I DIDN'T KNOW YOU WERE BORN IN BRAZIL!

Staying Healthy

The Rabbis of long ago taught us about Shmirat HaGuf — the importance of taking care of your health. They knew that staying healthy is important to living a good life.

Some healthy things I do for my body are _____

_____

Some not-so-healthy things I do for my body are _____

_____

Even people who take good care of their bodies sometimes get sick.

	A LOT	SOMETIMES	NEVER
I get sick	❑	❑	❑

The Torah tells us that Miriam got sick and her brother Moses prayed for her. Miriam later got better.

I ❑ have ❑ have not prayed for someone who is sick.

I ❑ do ❑ do not believe that prayer can help someone get better because

_____

_____

When I'm sick I like _____

_____

I don't like _____

_____

Sometimes sickness can be scary.
I was scared about sickness when _____

_____

My feeling about it now is _____

_____

Visiting the sick is a mitzvah. It's called Bikur Cholim.

I ☐ have ☐ have not visited a sick person.

It made me feel _____

_____

Things I'd like to do for a sick person:

☐ **Do chores for them**

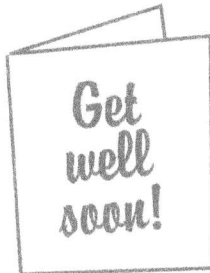

☐ **Make a special card**

☐ **Call them on the phone**

☐ **Read to them**

☐ **Run errands**

☐ **Tell them a joke**

☐ **Make something special for them**

MY OTHER IDEAS:

_____

_____

_____

_____

_____

49

Dear Diary,

My favorite things about spring are _____

_____

_____

_____

_____

IYAR / SIVAN
- Learn about Israel
- Eat falafel
- Have a Lag B'Omer campfire

During spring break I _____

_____

_____

_____

The weather has been _____

_____

_____

To celebrate Israel Independence Day we _____

_____

_____

_____

This month I went to _____

_____

_____

_____

_____

Dear Diary,

In my family we _____

_____

_____

_____

_____

_____

Shabbat is special when _____

_____

_____

_____

_____

_____

On Shavuot we _____

_____

_____

_____

_____

I'm looking forward to _____

_____

_____

_____

_____

_____

IYAR / SIVAN

- Read the story of Ruth
- Study all night (!) on Shavuot
- Eat dairy products

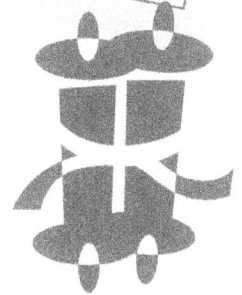

MITZVAH MEMO

I honored my parents

by _____

_____

_____

_____

Growing Up

Sometimes I wish I were younger so I could _____

_____

Sometimes I wish I were older so I could _____

_____

Being a teenager will be fun because _____

_____

Being a teenager might be hard because _____

_____

Grown-ups get to do fun things like _____

_____

Grown-ups have to do not-so-fun things like _____

_____

DO YOU THINK YOU'LL FEEL A LOT DIFFERENT WHEN YOU'RE THIRTEEN?

I GUESS I'LL STILL BE ME INSIDE!

Here is how I think I will look in the future:

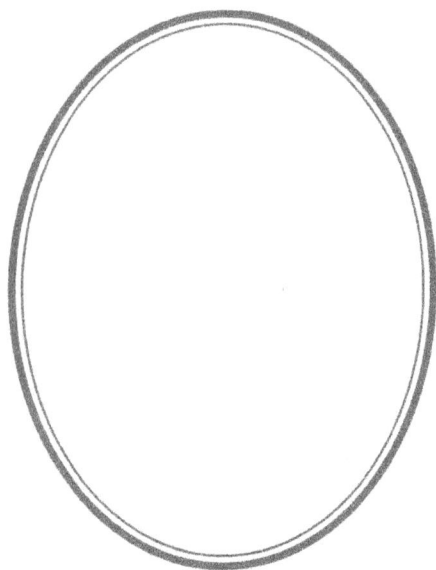

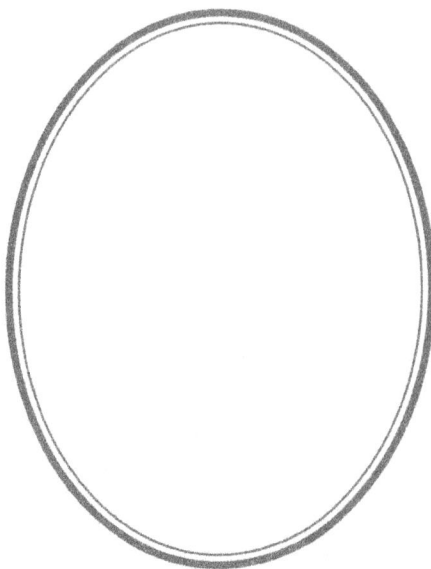

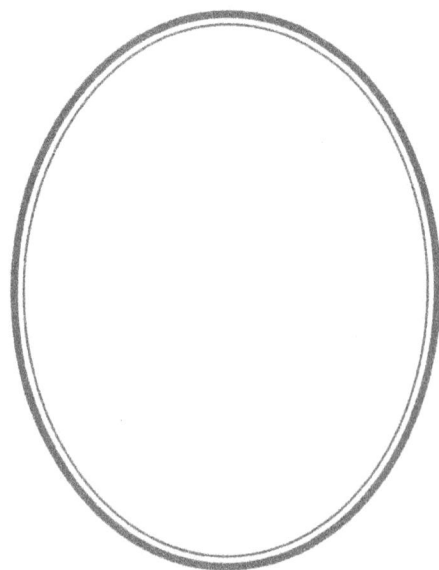

teenager   **grown-up**   **old person**

To get ready for Bar/Bat Mitzvah, I will have to learn

_____

I will invite _____

_____

I will know when I'm ready for Bar/Bat Mitzvah when

_____

After I turn thirteen, I will have more Jewish responsibilities,

such as _____

_____

I have been to the Bar/Bat Mitzvah of _____,

and I remember _____

MY FAVORITE PART WAS WHEN THE BAT MITZVAH GIRL READ FROM THE TORAH!

Here's how my Bar/Bat Mitzvah invitation might look:

front

inside

Life Cycles

We as Jews come together to mark happy and sad times in our lives — a birth, a Bar/Bat mitzvah, a wedding, a death. Our tradition tells us what to do at these life cycle events.

We celebrate a birth with a Jewish ceremony — a Brit Milah for a boy and a Brit Bat for a girl. This is when a child is welcomed into the Jewish community.

I ☐ have ☐ have not been to a Brit Milah or a Brit Bat ceremony.

I think baby ceremonies are _____

_____

because _____

_____

MY FRIEND AARON DOESN'T REMEMBER HIS BRIT MILAH!

How might someone feel at a baby ceremony?

THAT'S PROBABLY A GOOD THING!

	YES	NO	MAYBE	WHO MIGHT FEEL THIS WAY?
Happy	☐	☐	☐	_____
Sad	☐	☐	☐	_____
Scared	☐	☐	☐	_____
Angry	☐	☐	☐	_____
Silly	☐	☐	☐	_____
Serious	☐	☐	☐	_____
Embarrassed	☐	☐	☐	_____
Bored	☐	☐	☐	_____

TIMELINE OF IMPORTANT EVENTS IN MY LIFE

Write in things that happened and things you hope will happen.

My birth

MY PAST

The death of a loved one is a sad time. Judaism gives us ways to help the mourners — those who have lost someone close to them. For instance, Jewish mourners sit shivah. They stay home the week after the funeral, allowing friends to visit and comfort them. In this time, their house is called a "house of mourning."

I ☐ have ☐ have not been to a funeral or house of mourning.

I think funerals are _____

_____

because _____

_____

How might someone feel at a funeral?

	YES	NO	MAYBE	WHO MIGHT FEEL THIS WAY?
Happy	☐	☐	☐	_____
Sad	☐	☐	☐	_____
Scared	☐	☐	☐	_____
Angry	☐	☐	☐	_____
Silly	☐	☐	☐	_____
Serious	☐	☐	☐	_____
Embarrassed	☐	☐	☐	_____
Bored	☐	☐	☐	_____

MY FUTURE

Israel

The modern State of Israel was founded in 1948 in the land of our biblical ancestors. Israel is the Jewish Homeland — a place for all Jews to live in freedom.

KNOCK KNOCK!

WHO'S THERE?

ISRAEL!

ISRAEL WHO?

ISRAEL FUN TALKING TO YOU!

I ☐ do ☐ don't think it's important for Jews to have their own country because _____

_____

_____

_____

I ☐ have ☐ haven't been to Israel.

I think Israel is _____

_____

_____

A good reason to visit Israel is _____

_____

I ☐ do ☐ don't think Israel is the best place for a Jew to live

because _____

_____

_____

I ☐ do ☐ don't think every Jew should visit Israel because

_____

I ☐ do ☐ don't think I might make aliyah (live in Israel) someday

because _____

_____

_____

Things I'd like to do in Israel:

❑ Hike in the Negev

❑ Study Hebrew

❑ Float in the Dead Sea

❑ Eat at McDonald's

❑ Work on a kibbutz or a moshav

❑ Swim at the beach

❑ Visit the place where Abraham and Sarah are buried

❑ Celebrate my Bar/Bat Mitzvah

❑ Put a prayer in the Western Wall

❑ Take part in an archaeological dig

❑ Go snorkeling in the Red Sea

❑ Find the best falafel stand

❑ Make friends with Israeli kids my age

❑ _____

❑ _____

Draw a postcard from any time in Israel's history. Then write a message on the back. Who is the message from?

_____

Greetings from Israel

TO: _____

_____

_____

Jewish Food

Circle the holiday foods that you've eaten.

potato latkes

Holiday:

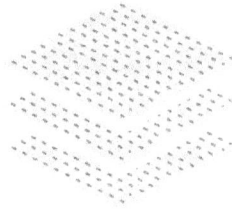

matzah

Holiday:

round challah

Holiday:

apples & honey

Holiday:

hamentaschen

Holiday:

charoset

Holiday:

horseradish

Holiday:

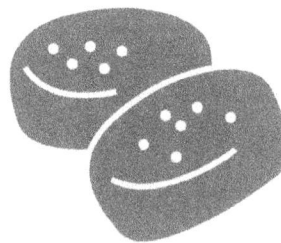

sufganiot

Holiday:

fruit & nuts

Holiday:

Are these Jewish foods?

Gefilte fish	❏ yes	❏ no	❏ maybe
Lox and bagels	❏ yes	❏ no	❏ maybe
Couscous	❏ yes	❏ no	❏ maybe
Shrimp cocktail	❏ yes	❏ no	❏ maybe
Corned beef	❏ yes	❏ no	❏ maybe
Falafel	❏ yes	❏ no	❏ maybe
PB&J sandwich	❏ yes	❏ no	❏ maybe
Chocolate	❏ yes	❏ no	❏ maybe
Pepperoni pizza	❏ yes	❏ no	❏ maybe
Chicken soup	❏ yes	❏ no	❏ maybe
Hummus	❏ yes	❏ no	❏ maybe
Hot dogs	❏ yes	❏ no	❏ maybe
Tsimmes	❏ yes	❏ no	❏ maybe
Ice cream	❏ yes	❏ no	❏ maybe
Potato chips	❏ yes	❏ no	❏ maybe
Salami	❏ yes	❏ no	❏ maybe
BLT sandwich	❏ yes	❏ no	❏ maybe

MITZVAH MEMO

I said a brachah before I ate _____
_____
_____

IS BIRDSEED A JEWISH FOOD? WHAT BRACHAH SHOULD I SAY?

These are Jewish foods I've helped make:

_____

_____

In my family, _____ does the grocery shopping,

_____ does the cooking, and

_____ does the cleaning up.

A Lot to Learn

Jewish tradition encourages Torah Lishmah — studying Torah for its own sake. Studying Torah can mean learning about Jewish history, language, and customs, as well as Bible stories.

Do you know anything about these interesting Jewish subjects? Check the ones you know about, and circle the ones you'd like to learn more about.

❑ Bible stories about battles

❑ The location of the Garden of Eden

❑ Israeli magazines for kids

❑ Children's stories from the Holocaust

❑ Bible stories about girls

❑ Jewish sports stars

❑ Rocks and minerals found in Israel

❑ Who designed the Israeli flag

❑ The location of Mount Sinai

❑ Bible stories about angels

❑ Jews in India

❑ How to make sufganiot

❑ Israeli pop music stars

❑ How to make a tallit

❑ How to figure out your Jewish "lucky numbers"

❑ Jews during the time of the Crusades

❑ Animals found in Israel

❑ Languages spoken by Jewish people

Ask your teacher to help you find books, videos, and websites to research these subjects.

TOP TEN LIST

These are the top ten things I learned in the last year:

1. _____

2. _____

3. _____

4. _____

5. _____

6. _____

7. _____

8. _____

9. _____

What have you learned about being Jewish from each of these?

Internet

_____

_____

books

_____

_____

videos

_____

_____

magazines

_____

_____

television

_____

_____

collections

_____

_____

travel

_____

_____

lessons

_____

_____

museums

_____

_____

I think "learning for its own sake" means _____

_____

_____

_____

Dear Diary,

My favorite things about summer are

_____

_____

_____

_____

_____

_____

We took a trip _____

_____

_____

_____

_____

A fun way to celebrate Shabbat in summer is _____

_____

_____

_____

The weather has been _____

_____

_____

_____

TAMMUZ / AV

- Go to Jewish camp
- Practice Hebrew during the summer
- Remember Shabbat on vacation

Dear Diary,

A Jewish book I read was_____

_____

_____

_____

_____

_____

I played these sports: _____

_____

_____

_____

I learned about Tisha B'Av. It is about _____

_____

_____

_____

_____

I'm looking forward to _____

Take your diary home and finish it during the summer.

MITZVAH MEMO

I took care of an animal by

_____

_____

_____

Wrapping It Up

Think back about your year. If you need a reminder, look back at the diary pages you wrote.

My handwriting is ☐ still the same ☐ different

It's different in this way: _____

_____

My favorite things are ☐ still the same ☐ different

They are different in this way: _____

_____

The best thing that happened to me this year was _____

_____

_____

Something I learned this year about being Jewish is _____

_____

_____

My favorite Jewish celebration this year was _____

because _____

_____

Date I finished this journal _____

MAZEL TOV!

YOU'VE FINISHED YOUR FIRST FUN JEWISH JOURNAL!